MAYA'S SONG

WRITTEN BY
RENÉE WATSON

ILLUSTRATED BY
BRYAN COLLIER

HARPER
An Imprint of HarperCollinsPublishers

April 4, 1928

Marguerite Annie Johnson was born on an ordinary day.
A St. Louis Wednesday caught between winter and spring.

Her papa, Bailey, loved her so.
Her mother, Vivian, loved her too.
Her brother, Bailey Jr., loved her most.
He called her Maya.

*She's my-a sister, my-a new best friend, my-a favorite person
in the whole wide world.*

A Black girl born in a world that didn't love Black girls,
born in a nation divided. White folks over here,
colored folks over there.

A Black girl born crying,
like all babies do.

Hush now, Maya's mother whispered.
Shh, Papa said.

But her brother, he didn't mind the noise at all.
Bailey let Maya cry as long as she needed.
He thought maybe his baby sister was trying
to tell him something.
Figured a baby girl crying so much, so loud
must have something to say.

Too Grand for His Own Skin

A proud man, an educated man.
Maya's papa spoke French and served in the navy.
Some of the white folks wanted Bailey Sr.
to shrink himself till his confidence
was as tiny as dust.
They wanted him to look down at the ground
when saying hello, but instead
he looked them in the eye, held his hand out to shake theirs.

Folks round town said Bailey Sr. was too grand for his own skin.
Black men who didn't know how to stay in their place
sometimes got spit on,
sometimes got beat, sometimes disappeared,
never to return to the people who loved them most.

So Maya's papa moved the family to California,
where he worked as a doorman
and got paid to shake hands
and look white guests in the eye.

Papa told Maya, *We are a people of dignity. Don't ever hold your head down*.

In California, Maya's papa could be grand, tall as the towering palm trees.
No way in the world they could make this grand man small.

No way in the world he'd fight overseas for his country,
only to come back home
and not be free.

One-Way Ticket

Maya was three years old
when her mother and papa's marriage ended.
Maya and Bailey were sent
to Arkansas on a train
to live with their grandma.

They wore tags on their arms.
In case you get lost, their mother said.
The train choo-chooed along,
leaving behind California's always blue skies
and no-snow Christmases,
leaving behind orange trees and lemon groves.

As soon as the train pulled into Stamps, everything looked different, felt different.
The yellow glow from the acid on the ponds, the way the air felt heavy and thick,
the Whites Only signs on the doors of stores, above water fountains.

Maya wasn't sure if she'd like it in Stamps. It didn't feel like home.
But she kept her head up, just like Papa taught her.

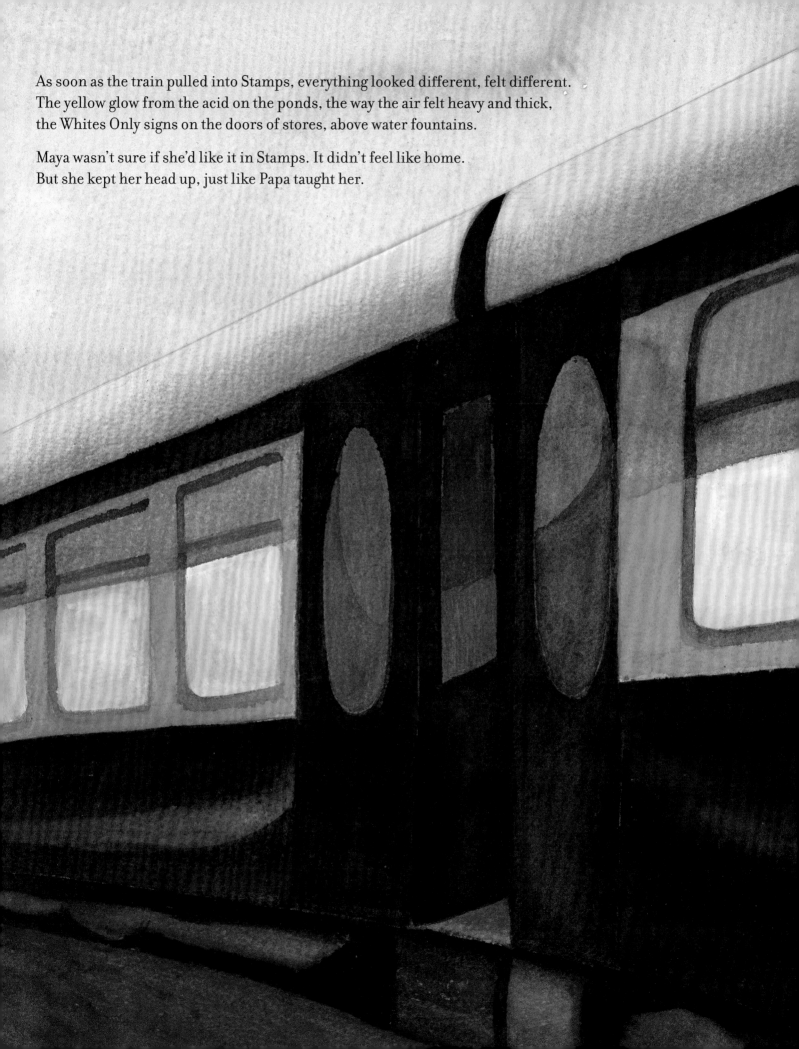

Miss Annie's Store

Everyone called Maya's grandma Miss Annie.
Maya called her Momma.

Momma never spent a dime
on anything but land.
She owned property that white folks lived on
and she owned a general store too.
No Whites Only signs here.
At Momma's store,
everyone was welcome.

In the early mornings,
just as the sun tickled the sky,
before the store opened,
Maya stood in the middle
of the lye-washed wooden floors
and inhaled,
taking in the smell of oranges,
onions, and kerosene oil.

She looked around at the shelves
stocked with too many items to count:
cans of sardines, boxes of soda crackers,
peanut patties,
all kinds of candies, thread,
and flower seeds.
Everything neatly stacked and in its place.

By the time the sun was in full bloom,
the store was a chorus of noise—
people going in and out,
the *ding ding* of the cash register.
Five cents for this, ten cents for that.

The store was more than a place for shopping.
This was the heart of town,
a place where Negroes came
for food to eat *and* to feed their soul.

On Saturdays, barbers set up in the shade of the porch.
The men told tall tales, trying to outdo each other.
Who was the bravest, who was the strongest?
Troubadours moaned their songs
and played cigar-box guitars.

Maybe living in Arkansas wasn't so bad.
Maya saw what love looked like up close.
She was in awe of the kind of miracle her momma was.
The daughter of former slaves and now
here she was
owning so, so much.

Sunday Mornings

Sunday mornings were for putting on handmade dresses and patent leather shoes.
Sunday mornings were for sitting on hard church pews, hymnal in hand, singing songs.
Sunday mornings were for shouting *Amen* and *Hallelujah* when the pastor said,
We are all God's creation and *God is love*.

On Sunday mornings, Maya had to hold in her giggles
when the women got to waving their hands and rocking
from side to side, when the deacon who couldn't sing
belted out a solo anyway.

Sunday mornings were for listening to the preacher say,
We've come this far by faith. Still got a long way to go.

Sunday mornings were for learning how to keep on going.
How to keep on and on.

When Letters Come Together

Momma had a friend who borrowed books from the white school.
Most things were better at the white school. The books were new and no pages were missing.
Momma used the books to teach Maya how to read. Maya practiced putting letters together,
making sounds and words that painted pictures in her mind, taking her to faraway places.

Maya buried the words of great poets and writers deep inside, deep inside.
Word-seeds from Shakespeare and Paul Laurence Dunbar.
Word-seeds from Langston Hughes and James Weldon Johnson.

A whole garden of words growing, growing inside.

Uncle Willie

His face drooped down on the left side,
his right hand bigger than his left.
He stuttered and limped and used a cane
and he knew how to do math.
He taught Maya her times tables.
Practiced with her day after day.

Come on, do your threes, now do your fours.

Maya recited her times tables like a song,
saying them faster and faster.
Uncle Willie would say, *You sure are a smart little girl.*
The smartest girl in town, said Bailey.

And on and on they went, multiplying numbers.
And on and on they went, multiplying their love.

When Night Came

The sun exchanged places with the moon. And when night came,
sometimes the white men on horses came too.
They wore white hoods, and one night, Momma thought they might harm Uncle Willie.
Maya and Bailey hid Uncle Willie in a crate and piled potatoes and onions on top of him.
When the Klansmen came looking for Uncle Willie, they couldn't find him.

Maya was proud of their clever idea, but surely whatever meal they'd cook
with those potatoes and onions would taste like sadness, like fear,
after being soaked in Uncle Willie's tears.

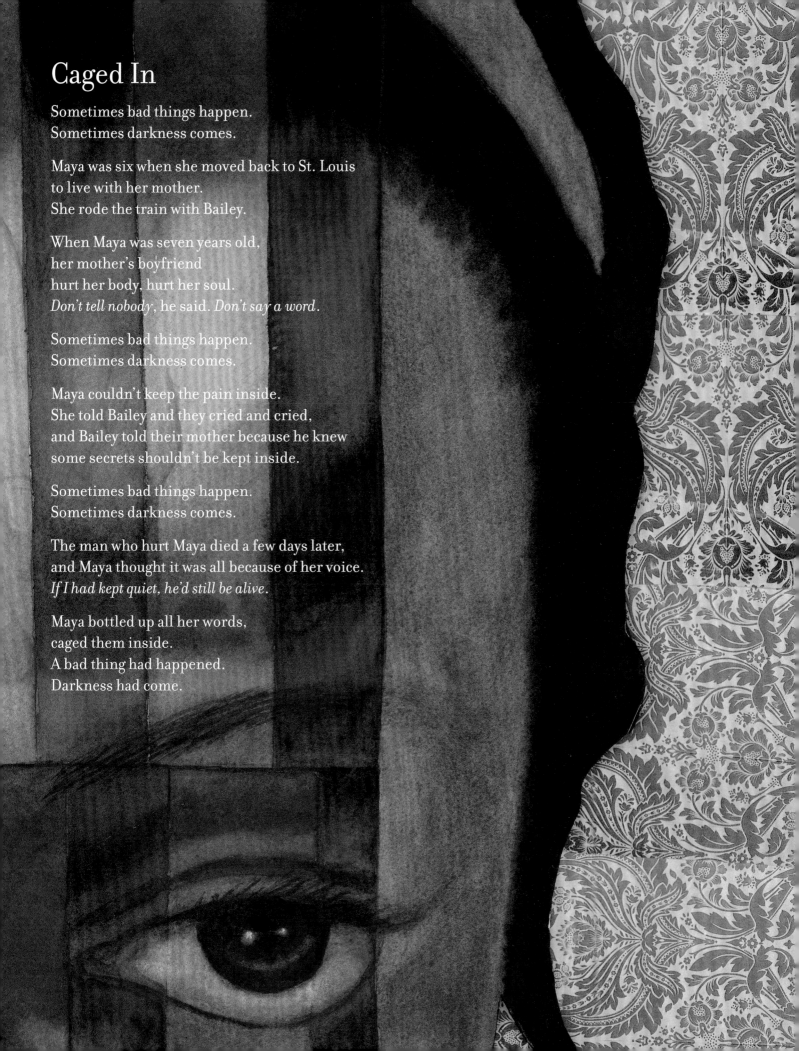

Caged In

Sometimes bad things happen.
Sometimes darkness comes.

Maya was six when she moved back to St. Louis
to live with her mother.
She rode the train with Bailey.

When Maya was seven years old,
her mother's boyfriend
hurt her body, hurt her soul.
Don't tell nobody, he said. *Don't say a word.*

Sometimes bad things happen.
Sometimes darkness comes.

Maya couldn't keep the pain inside.
She told Bailey and they cried and cried,
and Bailey told their mother because he knew
some secrets shouldn't be kept inside.

Sometimes bad things happen.
Sometimes darkness comes.

The man who hurt Maya died a few days later,
and Maya thought it was all because of her voice.
If I had kept quiet, he'd still be alive.

Maya bottled up all her words,
caged them inside.
A bad thing had happened.
Darkness had come.

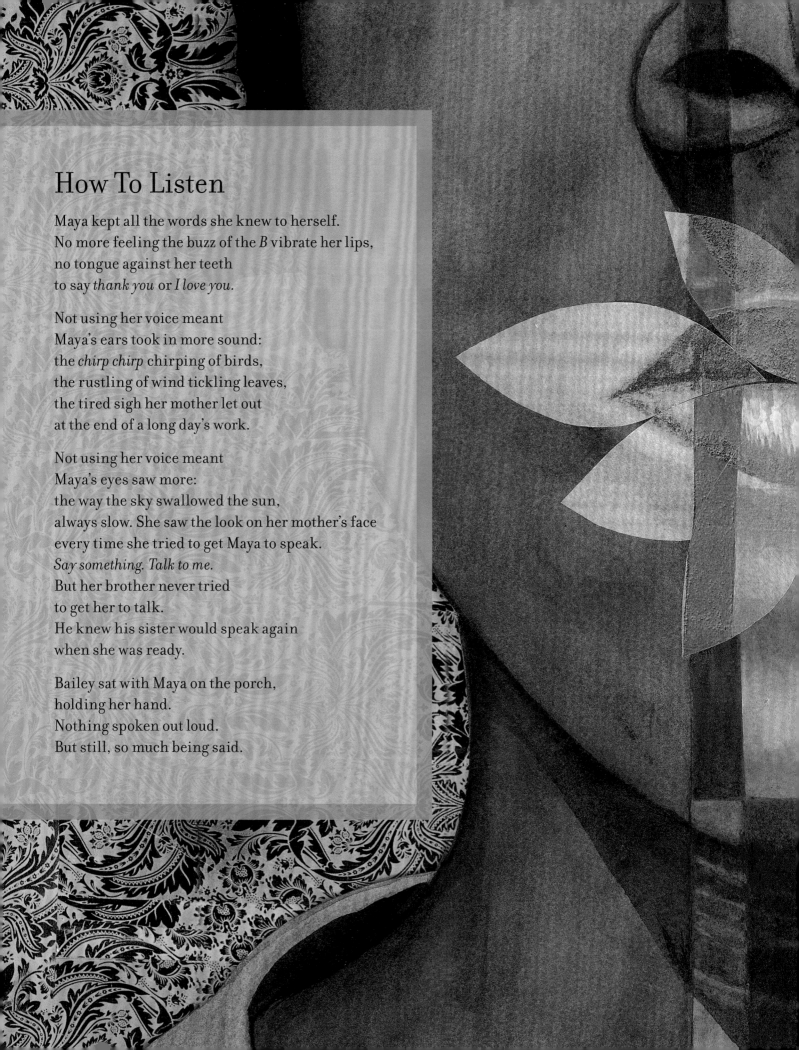

How To Listen

Maya kept all the words she knew to herself.
No more feeling the buzz of the *B* vibrate her lips,
no tongue against her teeth
to say *thank you* or *I love you.*

Not using her voice meant
Maya's ears took in more sound:
the *chirp chirp* chirping of birds,
the rustling of wind tickling leaves,
the tired sigh her mother let out
at the end of a long day's work.

Not using her voice meant
Maya's eyes saw more:
the way the sky swallowed the sun,
always slow. She saw the look on her mother's face
every time she tried to get Maya to speak.
Say something. Talk to me.
But her brother never tried
to get her to talk.
He knew his sister would speak again
when she was ready.

Bailey sat with Maya on the porch,
holding her hand.
Nothing spoken out loud.
But still, so much being said.

Another Goodbye, Hello

Maya's mother thought maybe returning to Arkansas
would take away Maya's sadness, so she sent her back.
Bailey went too.

Maya was excited to work at Momma's store again,
and she knew Momma wouldn't try to make her talk.

She knew Momma wouldn't expect anything from her
except love.

Silence

No words came out of Maya
for five years.

For five years,
hundreds of thousands of words came in.

What Momma Annie Said

While Momma brushed Maya's hair
and oiled her scalp, she whispered in her ear:

Listen, child, I know there's nothing wrong with you.
I know the good Lord just lettin' your voice rest
'cause he gonna have you usin' it all around this world.

Listen, child, you gonna be a preacher, a teacher.
You gonna travel this world, child, yes you are.

Once you start speaking again,
ain't nobody gonna be able to shut you up.

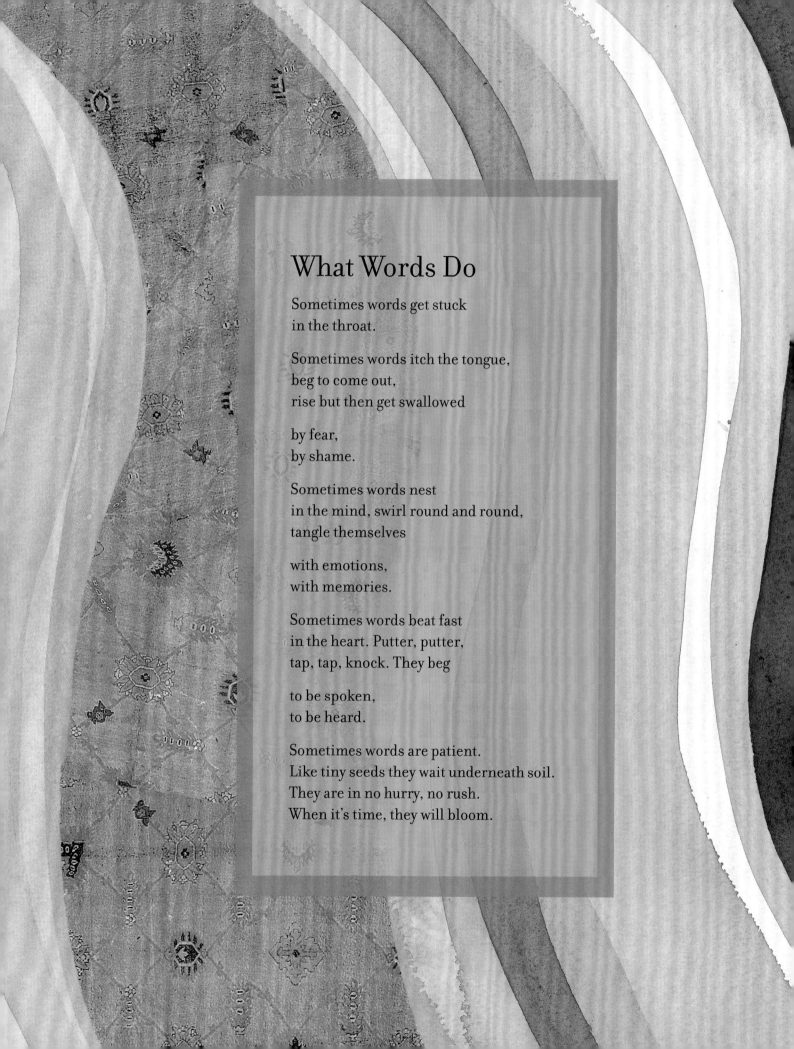

What Words Do

Sometimes words get stuck
in the throat.

Sometimes words itch the tongue,
beg to come out,
rise but then get swallowed

by fear,
by shame.

Sometimes words nest
in the mind, swirl round and round,
tangle themselves

with emotions,
with memories.

Sometimes words beat fast
in the heart. Putter, putter,
tap, tap, knock. They beg

to be spoken,
to be heard.

Sometimes words are patient.
Like tiny seeds they wait underneath soil.
They are in no hurry, no rush.
When it's time, they will bloom.

Poetry Is Meant to Be Spoken

Ms. Flowers, a family friend,
had Maya over for tea cookies and lemonade.
You gonna talk to me today? she asked.

Maya didn't say a word.

Well, if you won't talk, let's see what the poets have to say.
Ms. Flowers read poetry out loud to Maya.

Every time they read poetry together,
Ms. Flowers noticed Maya's smile, the light in her eyes.

Maya, sweetheart, you seem to really love poetry,
but you know, you can't really love poetry
unless you say it out loud.

Ms. Flowers told Maya, *You can't really love poetry till you speak it,*
till you let the words in you out.

Rebirth

Maya took a poetry book and ran
under the house where the chickens rested.
She sat on top of the soft dirt,
opened the book,
opened her mouth,
and words came out.

First in a whisper, then in a shout.
They leaped and danced
and bloomed out of her,
saying: *Listen, listen,*
we have something to tell you.

How to Build a World

Words poured out of Maya and she felt revived.
A whole world of words had been growing inside.

She believed people became what they said,
so she chose words carefully,
planted powerful affirmations in her world.

Words like *forgive*, like *kind*.
Words like *brave*, like *powerful*, like *phenomenal*.
Words like *faith*, like *dream*, like *free*.

Unexpected Blessings

Maya's world changed
when she turned sixteen.
In 1945, she had a son:
Guy Bailey Johnson.

Some folks around town
shunned teenage mothers.

But Maya's mother said,
*Life is always a gift
no matter when it comes.*

So Maya raised her baby boy.
Sometimes worrying,
Do I have what it takes to be a mother?

She told herself over and over,
Believe in yourself, trust you are enough.

This Is My Story, This Is My Song

To earn a living and provide for her son,
Maya wowed crowds with her singing and dancing
at the Purple Onion Night Club in San Francisco.
The audience knew jazz but what was this new music Maya was singing?

Have you heard of Calypso?
Listen to this Afro-Caribbean beat.
Sing with me, sing with me.

Maya brought Trinidad and Tobago
to California in every song lyric, in every note.
Her deep voice filled the room.
When the drums tap, tap, tapped,
Maya's bare feet moved across the stage.

Have you heard of Calypso?
Listen to this Afro-Caribbean beat.
Move with me, move with me.

Maya traveled with an ensemble of performers.
Sometimes they teased her because of her raspy, deep voice.
Maya's voice wasn't always pitch-perfect but it was always just right.
She refused to hold her head down, and sang louder and louder.
The little girl from St. Louis had taken her voice and her songs to twenty-two countries.
She traveled to Italy, France, Egypt, Israel, and Greece.
In Morocco, each of the performers were asked to sing a solo.
They all sang opera, but Maya chose to sing a spiritual
she learned as a little girl in Arkansas.

I am a poor pilgrim of sorrow
I'm lost in this wide world alone . . .
Sometimes I'm tossed and driven
And know not where to roam
I heard of a city called Heaven
I hope to make Heaven my home.

The audience gave her a standing ovation, and Maya realized
that even though she didn't have the voice others had,
she had her songs, her stories,
And that was enough.

Harlem

The place of Afros and raised fists.
The place where hundreds flooded the streets
to get a glimpse of Malcolm X
preaching and teaching.

Harlem.
The place of amateur acts at the Apollo,
jazz clubs and dance halls.

Harlem.
Lewis Michaux and the
National Memorial African Book Store.
John Killens and the Harlem Writers Guild.
Langston Hughes and his dreams.

Harlem.
A new home for Maya,
the place where she learned the power
of not only speaking words but writing them down.

Brother Jimmy, Brother Martin

Maya loved James Baldwin and Dr. Martin Luther King Jr.
with a deep, deep love.

They were more like sister and brothers than friends.
Jimmy was light in the darkest of rooms.
Martin was water in a parched desert.

Maya and Jimmy wrote about their experiences
living in America as a Black woman and man.
They were known all over the world, but when they were home in Harlem,
they were just two friends sitting at the kitchen table,
talking, debating, and loving each other.

Maya believed in Martin's vision.
She organized a musical revue called *Cabaret for Freedom*
and donated all the money to the Southern Christian Leadership Conference
to support Dr. King's dream.

Their friendship was an anchor. Kept them steady,
Kept them trusting that a change was going to come.
Freedom was coming, coming soon.

1962

Accra, Ghana.
Another place Maya called home.

In Accra, home was making kenkey with pepper sauce and fried fish.
Home was becoming fluent in Fante.

Home was teaching at the University of Ghana and
penning articles and essays for local magazines.

Home was learning from scholar W. E. B. Du Bois.
Home was having friends over for elaborate dinners
to talk about the happenings
in Africa, in North America.

Home was making new friends and welcoming old ones.

Home was preparing a feast for Malcolm X when he visited.
Home was sitting with Malcolm and listening to his new vision,
his plan to start the Organization of Afro-American Unity.

Maya loved living in Ghana,
but she wanted to be a part of Malcolm's movement.
She decided to leave Ghana and return to the United States
to join Malcolm.

Maya knew that home was never one place, with one kind of people.
Home was anyplace her voice could be heard.
Home was anyplace there was love.

February 21, 1965

When Maya arrived in the States, she made plans to see Malcolm
but before she could, he was assassinated.

Sometimes bad things happen.
Sometimes darkness comes.

Maya held on to Malcolm's words.
Maya . . . you can communicate because you have plenty of (soul)
and you always keep your feet firmly rooted on the ground . . .

Maya knew Malcolm believed in her,
so she would keep on and on.

April 4, 1968

Sometimes bad things happen.
Sometimes darkness comes.

Dr. Martin Luther King Jr. was assassinated
on Maya's birthday.

Coretta lost her husband.
Four children lost their father.
The world lost a leader.

Maya no longer had her friend.
Maya no longer had her joy.
Maya no longer had her voice.

For five days, Maya didn't leave her house.
For five days, Maya couldn't speak.

Rising

Jimmy refused to let Maya keep her words inside.
He took her to a friend's house for dinner.
After dinner, the guests gathered around Maya
and listened to her tell stories about growing up in Arkansas.

Every time one story ended, they asked for another.

Maya's stories were so good,
an editor, Bob Loomis, asked if he could publish them.

The world needs to hear your story.
No one can tell it like you.

Maya started writing her story down. She titled her first book
I Know Why the Caged Bird Sings.

She wrote about all of the joy and the sad times.
She wrote about all of the cities she called home.
She wrote about her family and friends
who were no longer alive to tell their own stories.

She carried them with her every time her pen touched paper.
She was writing her story and their stories too.

Good Morning

A cool, crisp day.
The sun a light glow.
Maya's words echoed across oceans,
blasted out of radios and televisions,
and hung over Washington, DC's sky.

. . . Give birth again
To the dream . . .
Each new hour holds new chances
For new beginnings . . .

It was the inauguration of President Bill Clinton.
He loved Maya's books and poems,
and he asked her to write a special poem for the nation.

Maya was the first woman
and the first Black person
to be given this honor.

Nearly thirty million people listened to her poem
"On the Pulse of Morning."

Maya's momma was right.
Maya was a preacher, a teacher.
A Black girl whose voice
chased away darkness, ushered in light.

Free Bird

Maya wrote her story in the form of autobiographies, poems, and songs.
She performed in movies and plays and gave lectures in many countries.

No holding her head down, no hiding. No more silence.
She didn't have the pitch-perfect voice others had,
but she had her songs, her stories.

And she alone was enough.

TIME

1928
Marguerite Annie "Maya" Johnson is born on April 4
in St. Louis, Missouri.

1931
Maya and her brother move to Stamps, Arkansas,
to live with their grandmother.

1945
Maya gives birth to Clyde Bailey "Guy" Johnson.

1952
Marguerite Johnson marries Anastasios Angelopulos and
officially changes her name to Maya Angelou.

1960
Maya Angelou works for the Southern Christian Leadership
Conference with Dr. Martin Luther King Jr.

1965
Maya's good friend and civil rights activist Malcolm X
is killed in Harlem.

1968
Maya's good friend and civil rights activist Dr. Martin
Luther Kings Jr. is assassinated in Memphis, Tennessee.

LINE

1969
Maya publishes her first autobiography, *I Know Why the Caged Bird Sings*.

1971
Maya publishes her first book of poetry, *Just Give Me a Cool Drink of Water 'fore I Diiie*, nominated for a Pulitzer Prize.

1977
Maya appears in the TV miniseries *Roots* and receives an Emmy Award nomination for Best Supporting Actress.

1993
Maya delivers a poem at President Bill Clinton's first inauguration.

2011
Maya receives the 2010 Presidential Medal of Freedom, the country's highest honor, presented by President Barack Obama.

2014
Maya dies on May 28 in Winston-Salem, North Carolina.

2022
Maya becomes the first Black woman to appear on the United States quarter.

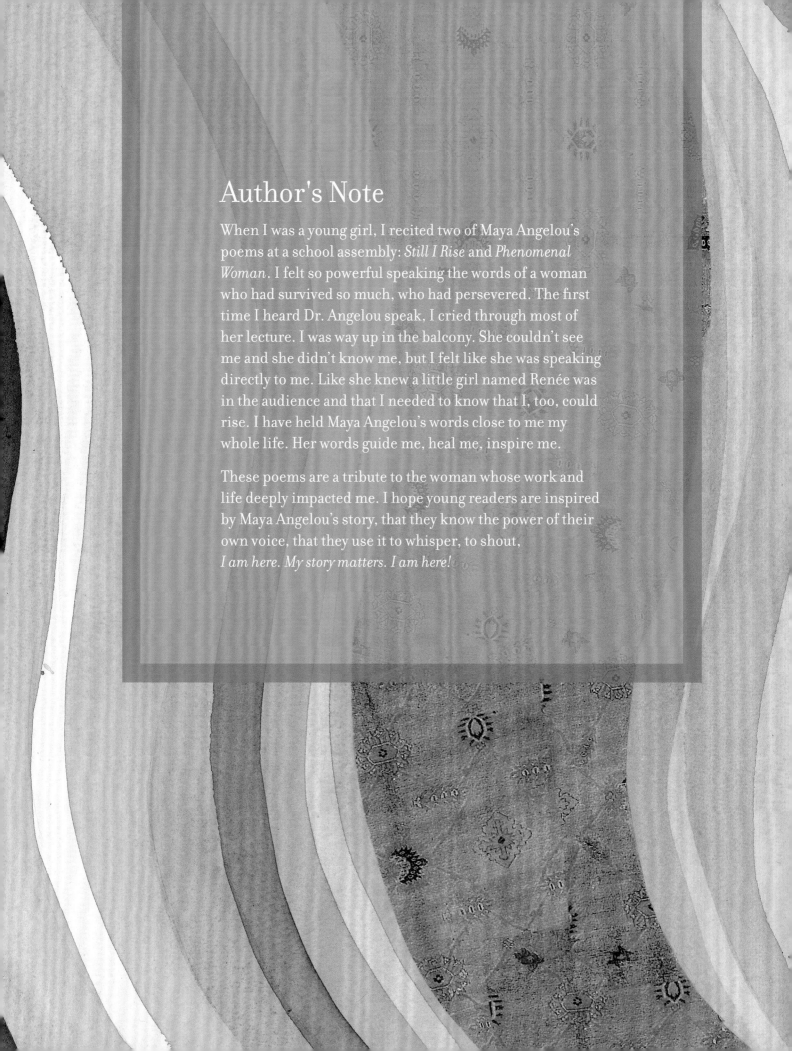

Author's Note

When I was a young girl, I recited two of Maya Angelou's poems at a school assembly: *Still I Rise* and *Phenomenal Woman*. I felt so powerful speaking the words of a woman who had survived so much, who had persevered. The first time I heard Dr. Angelou speak, I cried through most of her lecture. I was way up in the balcony. She couldn't see me and she didn't know me, but I felt like she was speaking directly to me. Like she knew a little girl named Renée was in the audience and that I needed to know that I, too, could rise. I have held Maya Angelou's words close to me my whole life. Her words guide me, heal me, inspire me.

These poems are a tribute to the woman whose work and life deeply impacted me. I hope young readers are inspired by Maya Angelou's story, that they know the power of their own voice, that they use it to whisper, to shout, *I am here. My story matters. I am here!*

Illustrator's Note

The story of Maya Angelou is one of inspiration and celebration, and her courage, honesty, and truth serves as a testimony to encourage us all to speak truth to power in order to overcome our adversities.

The book is painted in watercolor and collage and starts with young Maya and her older brother, Bailey, traveling by train to Stamps, Arkansas, to live with their grandmother.

Notice the use of certain colors (like blue) to express a sadness in Maya, and the brightness in color as Maya's mood changes to joy.

As Maya grew to fall in love with words, language, and song, she said it best: "And God put a rainbow in the clouds."

For these times we live in, I, too, embrace the idea that the power of light can always chase away the darkness.

A bird does not sing because he has an answer.

He sings because he has a song.
—Joan Walsh Anglund

For Kia Chatwaun Smith and Destiny Campbell —R.W.

I dedicate this book to all ages and encourage you
to be a rainbow to someone's cloud. —B.C.

Maya's Song

Text copyright © 2022 by Renée Watson

Illustrations copyright © 2022 by Bryan Collier

All rights reserved. Manufactured in Italy.

No part of this book may be used or reproduced in any manner whatsoever without written permission except in the case
of brief quotations embodied in critical articles and reviews. For information address HarperCollins Children's Books, a
division of HarperCollins Publishers, 195 Broadway, New York, NY 10007.

www.harpercollinschildrens.com

Library of Congress Control Number: 2022930115

ISBN 978-0-06-287158-9

The artist used watercolor and collage to create the illustrations for this book.

Typography by Chelsea C. Donaldson

22 23 24 25 26 RTLO 10 9 8 7 6 5 4 3 2 1

❖

First Edition